Clutching . . .
. . . Amber

John Alcock is a Birmingham-born writer and lecturer. Formerly a Lecturer in Drama at the University of Warwick, he returned after early retirement to become Director of Open Studies Creative Writing. A lifelong poet, he has a special interest in the performance of poetry, for which he won a Richard Burton Award. He is also a Housman Prize winner. He has been published, broadcast and given readings throughout the UK and USA. He lives near Stratford-upon-Avon.

Clutching . . .
. . . Amber

John Alcock

Silver Lake Press

Date of Publication:
September 2002

Published by:
Silver Lake Press

© Copyright 2002 John Alcock

Printed by:
ProPrint
Riverside Cottage
Great North Road
Stibbington
Peterborough PE8 6LR

ISBN: 0-9543195-0-8

CONTENTS

Proem: Backroad	1
Sitting on the stairs	
Listening Post	2
Wind-Waif	3
Betula Pendula	4
Touching Mould	6
Green Children (1)	8
Outer Circle 11	11
Sunday Lunch With Uncle Bill	12
Gongoozling	14
EGBDF	16
The Effects Of Aging On The Urban Motorist	18
Crushed petals	
Visiting Dominic	19
Gift	20
Pythagoras At The Angel	21
The Conjuror	23
Requiem For The Rose	24
Albert's Butterboxes	25
The cooling land singing	
The Dig	26
'Wounded At Waterloo'	28
Arbor Low	30
Catton Rough	31
Three Kings In Rutland	33
Dryden's Mirror	35
Skating Home	37
September Music	39

Somerset Rhynes	40

Take whatever dream you will

Legacy	42
Fools Gold	43
Mary Stanfield	44
Poet In Season	46
Thoor Ballylee	48
Sky Road	50
Roscommon Bog	52
The Callaun Quilt	53
Hanora At The Wart Well	55
Mothwords	57

Before the bus pulls out

Bagels For Breakfast	60
Apples Of My Eye	61
New England Patriots	63
Leaving Chicago	66
In Transit	67
Song Of The Senses	68
New Mexico Sundown	69
Clutching . . . *amber*	71
Mexican Hat Rock	72
Binoculars	74
San Francisco Soirée	76
My Life In The Movies	78
Malibu Blues	80

A distant radio
Last Tree To Paris	81
Svendborg Remembered	82
Somme	84
Buying Chocolate	86
Anamnesis	87
After Piraeus	89
Memorial Day	90

Forever bound by the picture's frame
Homage To Edward Hopper	91
Standing Back	92
At The Bathing House	93
Such An Ugly Subject	95
The Critics	96
Southwold 1937	97
Green Children (2)	99
Cherry Bend Creek	101
Like An Open Book	104
Trouble At A Tavern	105
Postscript: Take-Down	109

ACKNOWLEDGEMENTS

First and foremost, my thanks to The Cannon Poets of Birmingham for their encouragement, advice and support over nearly twenty years. Also to friends, colleagues and Open Studies students in the Dept of Continuing Education at the University of Warwick. To workshop leaders, especially Kate Clanchy, Gillian Clarke, David Hart, Deryn Rees-Jones, Peter Sansom and Jo Shapcott.

For interest shown in my work: the late Leonard Clarke (BBC), the late Eugene Haun (Eastern Michigan University), Edward Lowbury, the Afan Poetry Society, the Housman Society, the National Association of Writers in Education (NAWE), the summer schools of Essex LEA and the University of Toronto.

For publication and broadcasts: special gratitude to the editors of: *Broadside 1-1X* (Century House/The Cannon Poets) and *The Magazine* (U of Warwick). Also *British Poetry Review, Guild House Series* (U of Michigan), *Poetry & Audience* (U of Leeds), *Raw Edge* (West Midlands Arts). Anchor Books, Bloomin' Arts (Oxford), Forward Press, Frogmore Press, Penhaligon-Page, Poetry Today. Producers at BBC Radio 2, Radio 4, CW, WM. Festival directors of Birmingham Readers & Writers, Cheltenham, EMU (Hungry Ear), Forest of Arden, Ilkley, Ledbury, London (Running Horse), Port Talbot.

DEDICATION

TO MY FAMILY
for their love, encouragement, support
and just the right amount
of well-judged bullying

PROEM

BACKROAD

Gentled way, roll-wide,
offering a new step forward
and inviting; a stranger
taking me by the arm, indicating
the path to the lake I had
not noticed. Redpack mud
hard upon crusted pavement.

Woodchuck looks up in surprise
and why not? – we've never
seen either before. He
though, lives here, where
sunbeams bend between
stalks of sweetcorn high-to-heaven
around the lake edge.

White rail guides along trail
past boardhouse where someone
waves a hand from the stoop,
porchseat swinging; no matter
he's facing the other way – his home,
he knows who comes calling.

Was I meant to drive that road,
dirt-dust peeling off rear tyres
to fly over much-travelled ground,
leaving something of the fact
I am passing by . . .?

LISTENING POST

Sitting on the stairs
is where you view the world
from best as children know

Even as adult
you become the child again
nobody knows you're there

Squint through the banisters
from a safe elevation knowing
grown-ups never look up

Hear what the world says
you are not entitled to know
and anyway you should be in bed

WIND-WAIF

Cool, the air sipping treetops, blow
   down from the hill, dusting previous
heat off the parched road. Grass,
   blackened towards summer's end,
crinkles with lazy reflex beneath
   Kiltie sandal, new crêpe squashing
hurriedly by. Vision at turn of
   road-end, four years old, gold
hair cascading innocence. Twist
   of heart at that child world away,
rainbow-woven memories just stirring
   in wind's refraction. Dull edge of
mature mind aware that some
   small thing is already wrapped
in fledgling independence. Wanting
   has to become hoping: that
is the most any season will allow.

BETULA PENDULA

The 15 birch grove
correction 14
since my neighbour one day
butted his car into a tree
and in a fit of vengeful pique
hacked it down thus achieving
a run unimpeded to the village pub

The 14 birch grove
waves in mutual concord
celebrating a pastel April morning
and my eye is drawn
not to the shattered stump
of his spitefulness
but to one special *pendulum*

taller and more robust
and showering a premature catkin
greenness yet denied the other 13
as happens every year
this pack leader gracing
with accelerated seasoning
a remembrance I like to think

of the centre and prime
world of my children
bouncing and climbing
cheerfully on these chosen boughs
which continue to respond
with a special precocity
to the unforgotten laughter
of their growing pains

TOUCHING MOULD

is what you don't do
nowadays
instead
you press keys to encode
the load of your CD ROMp
peak through your WINDOWS
and only sometimes sing
color me virtual

so take your grubby
two-year-old fingers
and scrape leaf mould
while you can

puddle your toe-holed socks
in mounds of not-alloweds
before leafing by proxy
is all you have left

this way you'll establish
your entitlement
while you have lives enough
to buzz through

trample the world into turning
dab enough earth
to fill your mouth
know what it tastes like

scrabble fingers and toes   little one
and discover
how to make . . .

. . . scrumptious

GREEN CHILDREN (1)
Bournville Park, Birmingham

I think I know where the children are hiding
beneath the bank where the brook
runs shallow with pebble laughter
and the water digs caves
where the children may sleep

Still I think I know
having moved to a deeper place
the current reeding and weaving
festoons to catch coots' feet
growing sweetgrass and arrowroot
for the children to eat

This is no good
this was too long ago
yet I've come
from my serious meeting
and in an unexpected way
ended up here with my sandwich
and Styrofoam cup of soup
and I know they are still here

just as they used to be when I was one of them
and the girl and the boy we used to be
played here at weekends
walked home from school just old enough
to start saying rude things but not too loudly
for the laurels and sweeping laburnums
spied on us with teacher's eyes

That was when our skin was still green
its new translucency
stretched tight across carpus
and tarsus scarcely formed
though we skipped and smiled
and learned how to hold hands

But our green skin taught us to itch
in our school-stiffened clothes
till we cast them off and stood green
on the sandy brim shouting and daring
until the hot sun told us we could jump in

We were more like plants
than the plants in the park
dripping our foliage back to the bank
plants that could roar
and do dares and run away
and did not have to sit up all night
locked in the park when the gates were shut
as the poor plants did

Till the time when she did not come any more
though my parents would not say why
and I had to go for walks by myself
and try to think where she could have got to
among the roses giving nothing away
in their geometric beds
past rattling beech-leaved hedges
bordering paths which now for the first time
led nowhere and certainly not to adventures

But I knew I knew
she was somewhere there
my green companion
who much later I learned
had moved away to a world
no child should discover
my parents said
until they are older and I was too young
to understand so why bother
your young head you'll soon forget her

Though I never did
which is why I sit
today and listen to chimes
from the bells in the carillon tower
across the park
telling me in their coppery tones
to look for one who still swims
in the evening ripple
of my childhood brook
holding out her green fingers
for me to try to take
which only these words can reach

OUTER CIRCLE 11

Twenty-six miles
marathon distance
but we Olympians
preferred to rest our feet
upstairs for half-a-crown
'all the way round'

Kings Heath
Harborne
Erdington
exotic as Honolulu
or Cotapaxi
and we got home in time for tea

Commissioned by Birmingham City Council 1999
for display on Outer Circle buses

SUNDAY LUNCH WITH UNCLE BILL
For Hazell Hills – after T Kittelsen: *Princess with Bears*

My Uncle Bill was a bear:
he rumbled comfortably on Sundays
and smoked cigars only a bear could smoke,
once unpeeling the complete bear pelt
of a Havana leaf
and wrapping it round my arm
to show how warm a bear can feel.

From then on the Outer Circle bus
was full of bears and though
one wore a jaunty driver's cap
I sat upstairs in the front
and did the real driving
until we reached the park:

Warley Woods where all the bears
of Bearwood really lived,
hidden among the brambles behind the peacocks' cage,
though they never frightened me
any more than the Home Guard
on manoeuvres, pretending
to be invisible despite
large ursine khaki buttocks
protruding from privet hedgerows.

Sad that Uncle Bill the Bear
should die on a Vickers Viscount
coming in to land at Jersey airport
and never really met a naked princess:
I'd like him to have done that
and with what respect he would have treated her,
for he could smile
as only a real bear can smile.

GONGOOZLING

Uncles are best
at gongoozling

Aunts too impatient
their string bags
(which uncles never offer to carry)
too full of lemonade bottles
and spare socks

Coming gongoozling
uncle would say
and we'd be off
to the Odd Lock
to sit among willow herb
and kingfishers

See there's a boat (I'd cry)
*coming down from Lapworth
see how she swims*

But uncle would just stare
while I worked the lock
pushing my small bent back
against the beam

Ta lad boat woman would call
thar uncle's a right gongoozler
nodding her bonnet to him
who had not moved
though auntie slapped
meat paste disapprovingly
onto slices wide as paddles

The cut would settle and we
would chomp our sandwiches
in a kind of contemplation
scarcely heeding
old grey heron
silent and undisturbed
in the reedmace
spiking goggle-eyed bleak for tea

Maybe at that
herons make better gongoozlers
even than uncles

E G B D F

Sex was something
one probably did
in groups of six –
or so I supposed for
that was the number
of boys selected
at a time to follow
Father Kiernan on his
walks of instruction

Taking place on Sunday
afternoons mostly – during
recreation so perhaps sex
was meant to be quite fun –
Father Kiernan strode ahead
his words floating back
punctuated by dots
and question marks of smoke
from his discursive pipe

Sex had a lot to do
with seeds and the wind
it seemed which is why
the barley throve beside our path
in such fecundity – able
to propagate with an enlightenment
from his discourse which
threw mere mortal boyhood
into some confusion

That sex had something
to do with our own bodies
we grasped more by instinct
but that was only relative –
interest in our physical selves
being more centred upon
the rugger field and how to distinguish
the crunch of dislocated shoulder
from the smart crack of broken collar bone

The opposite gender
never really came into it
apart from improbable conjectures
after lights out – though
sisters could be mentioned
any time and other boys
would seem quite interested
as could one's mother though that
made one go slightly pink

Real girls would be encountered
somehow in the Sixth one knew –
somewhere between being allowed
to smoke after Compline
and having tea with
the Father Provincial
on his annual visitation –
and were therefore probably
quite important to one's future

THE EFFECTS OF AGING ON THE URBAN MOTORIST

From home to the skipping park
clutching a bag of scratchy crusts
for the snapping ducks
took four years

Today I drove it in 90 seconds

Coming home from school
kicking conkers
exhaling white breath
pretending to be
the world's heaviest smoker
took six years

Today I drove it in 3 minutes

Going to the grammar
learning to forge
parents' signatures on sick notes
spending whole lunch hours
mentally undressing the school secretary
and being immodestly good at English
took seven years

Today I drove it in 10 minutes 30 seconds exactly

Which perhaps explains why
from the reluctant perspective of late middle age
childhood sometimes seems to have lasted
barely a quarter of an hour

VISITING DOMINIC

They are the trails
these catalysts of tears
the shadow of footfall
on grey-silver dew

A time for weeping
those silent prayers
uttered to one unseen
but viewed with hope

Stepping at sunrise
where cloud is riven
looking for answers
in the broken sky

How else we plead
can ever come
a hoped-for assurance
a wished-for reply

GIFT

walking westward slow
from your grave on what
should have been your birthday

smudged crayon marks
of smoke pointing south
in almost-stillness

early December sunset
shooting the red-to-orange
with blue-green moire

rooks like so much
charred paper poised
in shapes of articulation

then the unexpected leather
thong of wingbeats whipping
rooftop air to turbulence

two swans navigating with
necks outstretched in taut
concentration of set purpose

your gift I am quite sure
your day making mine
unforgettable

PYTHAGORAS AT THE ANGEL
For A.L.R.

Geometry and I did not agree
at school, where the debating club
conspired to rescue me
from the hypotenuse; cricket
field my only assuaging square.

Why these thoughts today,
sat at the bar of Kingsland's
Angel Inn, set so many times
and distances away?

Time is no longer linear
we are told, though whether
it bends as Einstein hints
or hops from Hawking's hole
to hole is too much –
geometry to me.

At this corner of the bar
I am inclined to postulate
my own theorem: the past
at right-angles to the future,
as if the amiable ghost
of old Pythagoras were here
to tap me on the shoulder
uttering: 'At last my boy . . .'

The present, then?

Is where I perch
at the coign, glancing
along the old bar
to where you used to sit
at your iron-legged table,
pen as ever pricking
the surface of the novel
you were just about to write:
over a generation ago,
before our parting and
our setting out.

Now death has seen
to the collection
of your empty glass
who never did quite make it
to the corner where I turn
to face the new bar
('refurbished' in the trade)
you would not recognise,
giving access to a garden and,
beyond, my waiting car.

So drain my measure
and nod farewell before
hand into pocket for my keys –
only to be withdrawn
in sudden pain, a finger
stung, blood-beaded by
the lance, as it were,
of a hidden compass point.

THE CONJURER
For Peter Bailey, Poet

Winter is a great deceiver
spread like a magician's table
rigged with vacant boxes
and hollow cylinders
of unseen surprise
lying beneath the murk
and saturated gloom
of January days
until the conjurer taps
with mystic wand
declaiming magic spells
to make all clear

And who illusionist
other than poet
wafting pen as withe
to wave enchanted words
writing of life beneath
the sleet of dismal days
revealing the secret aconite
and catkin of the season's change
while we your readers
ooh'd and aah'd
despite your claim
you had nothing up your sleeve

REQUIEM FOR THE ROSE
Diana Princess of Wales, August 31 1997

Early to the window
that late summer morning
joy at the expectation
of the rose

Remembered in dream
recalled upon waking
the radiant blooming
of the rose

Drawing back the curtain
shock of seeing
the keen cut stem
of the rose

Tearfully gathering
a few crushed petals
last spoiled remnants
of the rose

Yet still there lingers
all through the garden
the consoling fragrance
of the rose

ALBERT'S BUTTERBOXES
Model of Worcester Cathedral
made by Albert T Harley
between March 1977 and June 1984

I envy Albert his economic perception
'nothing waste' he would say at breakfast
scraping the last lick foregoing marmalade
carefully placing the empty butterbox
to one side behind the coffee pot
'There's the North Porch' he would say with satisfaction

And I think how I have lacked economy
been so wasteful disregarding scraps
why only this morning I threw away a carton
emptied of orange juice when it might have been
a pinnacle final glory of a tower
and have denied someone a topping-out ceremony
because of my impatience too quick to discard

So Albert took his time his 15,300 hours
while I have lived over 22,000 days
and left my litter of discarded shirts
worn-out shoes unreplied-to letters
thousands of gallons of water from the shower
and friends lost somewhere (surely this is the worst)

I look at Albert's model and learn my lesson
that nothing need be wasted nothing be lost
but my hands must form the beauty from the dross
as Albert's fingers probed despite arthritic pain
and Albert's wife no doubt would smile as she added
another box of butter to her shopping list

THE DIG
Wootton Wawen, Warks 1975

And those feet did
in ancient times walk,
caper or falter over the glebe land;
bones of lemon-colour
delicately trowelled into view,
tagged and numbered
for second interment
in the *Transactions of the Society*.

This afternoon of early dark,
with huddled archaeologist
back in her caravan brewing tea
(just a splash of brandy),
splaying red-raw fingers
to the electric ring,
the mist assumes limbs of light
proportion, hand proffered
to wraith-extended hand
as the slow dance begins.

We, at eight centuries distance,
keep common time, conversing
in silences to the measure
of our shared vision: did he,
in some wild dream, perceive
my coming so long after
the inestimable time of his obsequy?
Could I call to one an equidistance
forward, treading across yet unborn time?

2775: the number jolts the page
and struggles in the mind arhythmically;
yet this is the gorge
we seek to bridge tonight
while cars cut corners yards away
anxious to risk a minute saved.

Tonight I share with one who was
and call to one who may look back to me:
   Dig me up too in my time
   and listen; even I may have
   as much to tell you.

'WOUNDED AT WATERLOO'
Henry Houghton, wounded June 18 1815
buried at Wootton Wawen, Warks

Those words cut deep
in Wilmcote stone
proclaim a legend
among our country tombs
contrasting with
'Called Home'
'Asleep in Jesus' Arms'

For home and sleep did not come easily
to one whose teenage zest
was circumscribed by years
of cutting pain
and sudden-waking screams
of blood and blade
and comrade falling

Your wounds slow-healed
who lived to tell a tale
for all to wonder at
till doubtless younger ears grew bored
with ale-embellished talk
of times long gone
and battlefields grown cold

Until your death
forever silenced words
and long-dim victory
became consigned
to some prolix official history
lacking the combustive charge
of grape-shot tempering bone

'Wounded at Waterloo'
must take its place
beside our village cross
to world wars' slain
uniting Dunkirk and Passchendaele
with Agincourt and Senlac Hill
in a continuum of sacrifice

ARBOR LOW
'Derbyshire's Stonehenge'

The ravens remember
when the stones lay down
to sleep their way
through the gathering storm
among cloud-clipped hills
chopped and ordered
into stone-walled pastures

> *The tribes*
> *the blood sacrifices*
> *the cut jugular*

Today is bleak enough
to throw caution
to the smarting winds
walk beyond
the tyre-battened stench
of the Farm for Sale
nobody wants

> *The concealing ditch*
> *the chieftain's lust*
> *the crazy-veined cattle*

Plod across thistle sting
to salute the stones
content to see out
our cartoon celebrations
wysiwyg images
awaiting their fifth or sixth
(having lost count) millennium

CATTON ROUGH

Mouthful of pebbles
sour to the tongue
even the rough edge
of sheep lick

Brackish the water
blackish the draining
between spiked roots
of Blackthorn

Flood-plain Crowfoot
emitting signals
soaked flares
of distress

4-wheel slosh
against all odds
search for stray lambs
ditch-delivered

Scratched horizon
of skeletal alders
beating the bounds
on the bailiff's dry run

Sweat dripping heat
to deliver ewe
crawl like an old bitch
belly to ground

Wall-eyed dog runs
teg with wether
folds fleece to thistle
snip go the shears

THREE KINGS IN RUTLAND

Red road
balancing unsteadily on the shoulder
of the black hill
wavers like a child on a first bike
and spills
onto the flat green valley floor

Meanwhile
they have forded the stream at full flood
the three figures
pursuing an imperturbable course
in line ahead
or echelon as the whim takes them
halting a moment in silhouette
against the parodying tonsure of tree fringe
on the hill's top

THREE
MAGNIFICENT
FIGURINES

Disappearing into a grove
to emerge over plough and continue
unflinching toward field-flood
unscathed by hedgerow
slipping between hawthorn stems
like smoke

THE PURPLE KING
THE ORANGE
AND THE PEACOCK

Moving across a sepia landscape
in the dun rain of late afternoon
procession moving
inevitably towards the water
of the reservoir
this witness wanting
to run forward with warnings
but held back until
no more is visible
in the lake swirl
than a sudden reflected flash
of late sun as if

a bright new star had just been born

DRYDEN'S MIRROR
Canons Ashby House, Northants

'Queen Elizabeth slept here'
has never impressed me much
though these English midlands
are more likely to have found
Charles 1 and Cromwell vying
for sleep in a stranger's bed amid
the rampagings of their ungodly war

Surely someone would have
changed the sheets since when
the royal sweat besmirched
stale linen sniffed with relish
by egregious minor lords
hoping their B&B proclivities
would bring them rich preferment

Here within the rambling walls
of Canons Ashby though
the artefacts of age and honour
display a different feel
and one in particular draws me back
to take a second look

Above the fireplace in a grainy hall
I see my own reflection caught
in a bloomed and mottled mirror
silvering turned to leaden pewter
the glass now liver-spotted
like the backs of aged hands

So that I doubt for a moment
the reflection is my own
staring back from that same
archivist of images
that once held Dryden's stare
pausing to correct the set
of his peruke or rehearse
a few more lines to Absalom

And even as fancy seeks to blend
our separate counterparts into some
strange overlay of physiognomy
perhaps a ghostly third pre-figures
both of us as Spenser passes
softly towards his chamber to pen
further stanzas to his *Faerie Queene*

A sovereign who may slip
at any time she chooses betwixt
the sheets of time dividing
yet conjoining each of us
on this late amber autumn afternoon

SKATING HOME
For Barbara

The geography of Cambridge fens
lies left and right
of familiar motor roads,
dripping north-east
towards the Wash,
while Peterborough's low cathedral
crouches with ears pricked up,
a friendly mutt
sniffing towards the Lincoln wolds.

Over the blanketed fens
a slow moon rises
to light the lanes
and empty country roads
blocked by heavy Ural snows
while the city evening motorcade
jostles and jerks, pumping
its poison breath with frustration
at getting nowhere.

History has hidden an old mobility
across this gliding landscape,
where reeds in huddled fathoms lie
in ice that once bit deep
at ears and swaddled toes
as scythes were laid aside
and secret journeys began,
skating with iron and bonded wood
towards home and fire and evening beer.

The motor exodus in multi-voiced
commuter chorus has drowned forever
the scrape and slice of skates,
reapers and cutters jinking
along the music staves of ditch and drain,
so many quavers jigging home
by Tick and Turf
and Bury Lug,
under the brimming stars.

Tick, Turf, Bury Lug: names of fen drains

SEPTEMBER MUSIC
Aldeburgh: in memoriam Benjamin Britten

Seaward the chant sounds
the cooling land singing
the end of the season

A darkness hangs under the sun
wings of air
beating time to the gulls' cry

Pebbles smatter across shingle bank
kicked by children racing
home – against the tide – from school

Last beachcomber trudges back
towards the timpani town
where shops have all closed early

But in your mind Ben
you heard the light now scarcely visible
leaping into harmonies of space

listened to stars manoeuvre
and spheres articulate
the sad beauty of September music

With thanks to Edward Lowbury

SOMERSET RHYNES

Sunsetting lightshow
pours golds and reds
over the Somerset rhynes

fingers of field drains
flexed and poised
to play as on a harp
the intricate scales
of pastures drowned
by Axe and Brue
  Carey
  Isle
  Parrett
Tone and Yeo
these seven rivers
inscribed forever
on the manuscript cover
of each winter's concerto

the harp to which
Alfred sang
in far off Athelney
his ragged army
wading waterlogged
to Muchelney
and Creech St Michael
cursing their short cut
through North Curry
for being flooded
not by nature's seasonal
activity but fishermen

hooked and netted
on tench and bream
acknowledging
only independence
from Saxon and Dane
and hungry abbot alike

I think that was all
a long time ago
though nightjars
rails and grebes
still counterpoint toads
burping their love calls
across the deep rhyne drains
as evening steals
across the smoky fens
and Alfred's ghost flits
along the sphagnum walks
as siren gases rise
and field mist lurks
bearing the musky smell
of evening smur

or cooking fires
or even the taint
of burning cakes

Rhyne (pron. 'rheen'): drainage ditch

LEGACY
Capel-y-ffin, Powys

Take with you the green mountain,
the gift of the green mountain;
cast for dark footprints in the lane
among the tumbled abbey stones.

Take eyes – my eyes if you would –
for the inner seeing; putting doubt
out of sight, walking so late
under the owl's-eye moon.

Take whatever dream you will,
whatever dream the mountain gives
to the inner eye, scanning, as buzzards do,
the cortex of granite and grass.

Take the heartbeat I once left
for safekeeping in a kingfisher's bolt
above the Capel stream; though older
it will still pulse strong enough for two.

FOOLS GOLD
For the Afan Poetry Society

Wedding rings for royals
lie deep in the mines of Clogau
hacked from the fingers
of long dead forests

My gold is easier to find
patined on the underside of rocks
brooded over by the Great Worm
guarding the Gower strand

Worthless on the international market
hewn only by beachbums
it still glints bright as a ransom
in my fool's eyes

MARY STANFIELD
Excommunicated 1829

Girl, why do you weep,
flinging yourself into
the docks and nettles
of my long-gone home;
I, Favonius, centurion
and long-dead dad
who would comfort
your rage if I could?

Your crime – if such it was –
and punishment were 'so unfair'
you said, exactly as my daughters would
in Fabriano when
I took them home early
(always too early)
from Nemesis' festival.

Driven by that grim
paternal council from
the Baptist congregation
because you danced:
three times on Sundays
you passed, with shoulders slouched,
the bright Bull Inn to hear
black words preached in shadow.

Till one jaunt proved too much:
a prayer and a coin tossed
into the collection plate
and you were off to find
the dazzled face of Ieuan ploughboy
and laughed and danced –
as they have said in their indictment –
'upon the floor of the Old Bull's Head.'

Oh, Mary, stand up;
though my silly tomb
is still gawped at by strangers,
you are the one they'll remember
as warm and alive,
who danced in Caerleon
one bold Sunday evening
for all womankind.

POET IN SEASON

As a young Irish poet
he lodged in London
feeling very alone

Get out and about
get to know some people
his landlady said

So having an uncle
who trained on the Curragh
he went to Ascot

dressed for the occasion
in a new green T-shirt
(with shamrock motif)

denim flares freshly pressed
knee patch neatly stitched
and of course obligatory top hat

He didn't quite make
the royal enclosure
but did know about horses

because of his uncle
and told some girls
and their horses won

so he was a hero
a hero and a poet
and they loved him and said

oh Seamus one day
you'll be famous but he said
not Seamus and they said

we know just our little joke
but could you oh could you
he assumed read them poems

so pulled from his pocket
his new little book
but they said *that's great*

but could you we're well thinking
since you're so clever
and famous already

please get us some tickets
        for Wimbledon
                instead

THOOR BALLYLEE
The summer home of W B Yeats

   That I am here
sitting on *the winding stair*
cheek pressed against
the circling wall
with its soda smell
grained in the granite blocks

   That he once trod
upwards and downwards
coming in over
the mud-tracked bridge
hauling his tired mind
to the battlements
breathing soft air
clean from the Atlantic
before descending refreshed
to his waiting family

   That somewhere above me
a taped actor booms his poetry
in endless repeated loops

   That somewhere below
someone is preparing
omelettes and lentil soup

   That on the second floor
I looked through the bedroom's
casement window at sitting-still
upstream-paddling ducks
and the whole tower
became my boat swimming
steadily towards the past
in a muteness broken only
by water sallies
and an occasional voice
which could by then
have been Yeats himself shouting
for pen nibs and fresh ink

   That a mottled sun breaks through
as suck of airbrakes brings
a tour of American academics
to a halt in the hidden parking lot
by the ford and the scattering coots

   Sums up this place
where among the pebbles
and stirabout mud
plated trout blob and grin
skimming their tinfoil scales
just below the surface
of the stream
confident that they are poets too

SKY ROAD

I celebrate the road and I sing the road
    Sky Road
sealing the Connemara coast
out of Clifden beckoning us on
towards Claddaghduff
Cleggan and Streamstown Bay
    to abide
At Bridie's cottage by Ballynakill

Smoke streams below
from a good home farm fire
coastguard helicopter chattering
across loop and spur
    coming in
from keeping an eye
on its precious investment
pearl-sheened Atlantic shore

Sure as Echdae the Sky Horse
flew above the Twelve Bens
    we scissor
the gravelled twists
in our gradient climb
and float the far side
    on wings
preened to coast our descent

Turf worn smooth as a Dunlin's egg
        bounces light
back at an ochre sun
taunting the tide to peel
off to a far America
where the bad spud once spat
so many of our ancestry
out to sea in their famine boats

Back in Bridie's kitchen
we dig in to scalded pork
and with a ransacked quaff toast
        a wedding party
safe back from Inishbofin Isle
singing the praises of the Sky Road
        set ever to defy
the laws of time and gravity

ROSCOMMON BOG

The road hops and skimbles
through the steering wheel,
bone drubbing rhythm
on a boghrán's goatskin hide.

Wrists and elbows braced
to keep the car on the shale,
evening air dashing windscreen
with slants of rain.

The turf cutters slog on,
working late at their slicing,
lifting, stacking and roofing
to hasten the drying-out.

A wave of a hand and a back
soon bent again to the task
that is forever trashing their land,
earning a fading living while they can.

Boghrán (pron. 'bow-rawn'): a tambourine-like drum
Runner-up, Housman Prize 2002

THE CULLAUN QUILT
For Diana, Jane and Kay at Warwick

October fog walls and banks
along Lake Cullaun's shore,
shutting down perspectives
of hidden water lapping.

You perceive your place
by instinct,
your bounding setter
sharing the freedom
of secret wanderings.

Later you stitch these images
in careful squares of moire,
glistening in the morning silks
of the quilt now stretched
and anchored to its frame,

holding memories still needle sharp
of sickness and bereavement
(as you've said),
even the gambolling
of your dog now set
in permanent memorial.

Later still
I view your finished work
displayed in the exhibition hall,
seeing spread before me
in white and gold and grey
the hues and tacks
of Cullaun-captured dreams.
Perhaps one day

you'll lie beneath your quilt,
wrapped in the weft
of hope and joy which I perceive
come shining through
each thread despite
those crewelled sadnesses.

The quilt, *October: Early Morning, Cullaun Lake,*
woven by Alison Erridge.

HANORA AT THE WART WELL
Timoleague, County Cork

Because the only track
told them to go there
rather than the beckoning of God
or the sea pounding its many voices
told them to stop
they knew they had found the place

Now that they were here
they built their church
cutting blocks
from the quartz-glazed rock
and worshipped a Lord
hewn by gales from winter ice

Imagine their beards in the wind
hands clutching patched habits
lips flickering candles of prayer
as they fed the souls of their flock
plunged bodily ills free from taint
into the wart well

Perhaps it was the coarse sea-grass
that proved too bitter
and not the feuds of chieftain
and absent abbot that moved them on
leaving the priory to unburden itself
of encumbering window and roof

Where does not matter
nor why
for there is only perpetual now
as the tides flow along the estuary
and above my head
the constant spiral of stars
which art in heaven

I who was once Hanora
lying beside Cregane
and Patrick and James
in the nave which is become
our nettled and hallowed grave
beside the wart well dry
as a drained communion cup

If was the once-upon-a-time
that brought us here
the expectation we came to depend on
the *if* we hoped
would prove to be
our everlasting *Amen*

Thanks to David Hart for his *keywords*
Worcester Cathedral 2001

MOTHWORDS

surf booms
along shoreline
moon lies back
enjoying

how can mothwings
beat so loud
dive into foam
roll back and ride

still   the   moth   wings   beat

heart drives motors
inside skull
tides fall and rise
tides tell moth
to fall and rise

and   rise

powdered membrane
carrying messages
fizzing like satellites
bouncing messages
above the saltsmash

moth mouth
has something to say
wing finetuned
if only you will listen

*

seacold
sparks of snow
inhabit the air
all about
sun catching finesnow
in suspension

blue shadows mark
crunch of each indent
at footfall
step by step measuring
cliff trail
mind and eye
alert to sky filled
with . . .

mothwings

*

ocean drums deep
more asleep than awake

cormorants safely
close an eye

halfglow greying east
tells *soon*

wind before dawn
remembers a dream

lighthouse
starts to attract attention
but sweeps away
in time

*

only in boeings 747
lights pinholing
in place of stars
is there some life
yawns registering
once passing interest
as in-flight movie
rolls closing credits

how we travel
as in a dream
wake to a dawn
over one land or another
joined by travellers
radar fails to signify

companions
who have kept pace
nightlong

*

mothwings
having no body
to manoeuvre
become messages
strong enough
to cross oceans

forever

Written on the Atlantic seaboards of Cornwall and Massachusetts

BAGELS FOR BREAKFAST

'One day,' the small boy said,
'I'll stand up there.' Now man
in later years he sees his firmament
below, a thin moon bathing
in the lake in Central Park.

A million earth-stars,
seeds of the Big Apple,
illuminate this childhood
promise, kept on a Manhattan
evening fast descending.

Twelve-hundred-fifty feet
of elevator rides to look
down from the Empire State
on knife-slice of Fifth Avenue,
grey sluice of Hudson.

Tomorrow the great wide
corridors of the mid-west,
forward drive selected
in pursuit of further ambition,
but first, bagels for breakfast.

APPLES OF MY EYE
Ann Arbor Michigan

Even apple picking
in the orchards along Zeeb Road

even the crush of juice
drooling from the cider press

even the russet sun
like a last overlooked apple

no compensation
for homeward longing

in the weekend sorties
of lonely intercalation

between bouts of imbibing
that 'much in demand' celebrity

conferred by research grants
on the academic visitor

Therefore to place of refuge
this maple-blazed afternoon

downtown bookstore
to hide among consoling shelves

only to spot mid idle leafings
one volume familiar from home

imported author causing
mind to quaver hand to shake

knowing these pages to enfold
images of my children

likenesses to gaze upon
with gauzing eyes while they

smile back to me garlands
fit to hang on apple boughs

NEW ENGLAND PATRIOTS
For Clare, Dom and Mal – the true patriots

Travelling with my children
in New England

I am conscious of being
the literary scholar

with a mission to fulfil,
a personal odyssey

that will become a minor
anecdote

retold in seminars to politely
bored students.

For I am on the fourth
and final leg

of a private pilgrimage –
that much

the children can just about
tolerate,

indulging father's whim –
to Rockport

Massachusetts, petite
and pretty

with apple blossom between
whiteboard

      seafront houses, windows mirroring
              Atlantic dawn,

        to view the Dry Salvages,
      setting of Eliot's third *Quartet*

            and reason
        for my journey, pride

             of fact
I have visited the English three locations,

        Norton, Gidding and ashes-
            laden Coker.

        My children though have
           other thoughts,

      Eliot coming nowhere in their
             reckoning

      beside the Bee Gees and John
             Travolta,

      current pounding heroes on
             our stereo

    as we swathe down Highway 95
               past

          Mystic and Salem,
            pausing only

to buy milk and local maps –
driving on

in sullen silence now
because

we could not pick up the black
and ragged stray

my daughter fell in love with
at the covered bridge.

In the event perhaps they
knew best:

The Salvage rocks, though
saw-toothed

and foamy backed, were
disconcertingly

less memorable (literary even)
than lobster grill,

saltwater taffy and a nest
of baby cottontails

we found that day, that spring
in Massachusetts.

LEAVING CHICAGO

Look starward downward
spread in clusters
from far horizon
across this blazing city

Night sky inverted
interstellar framework
transposing heavens
drawn down by mirrors

We climb through
cloud tissue
penetrating new strata
strobing upwards

Leave mock lunar
scoops of freeway
targeting real moon
slicing over our plane

Drawing us on towards
numberless candle-
lit runways where
only the mind can land

IN TRANSIT

Surely you have been there
sometime, waiting aimlessly
for the rain to stop,
your back thrust
against the grey wood
of an empty clapboard house,
seeking the brief comfort
of standing aside
from the direct line of fire.

Maybe you arrived by bus,
hump-backed Greyhound
squelching to a stop
in some unbaptised Midwest town,
travellers hopscotching
to coffee stands, buying magazines
and flexing creased muscles
before the bus pulls out
and leaves you.

Well, you were left standing
and, if you noticed, I was probably
hunched in some corner,
reading a paperback selected
from the dross of a three-faced
five-tier rack, wanting to run up
to whoever you are, longing
to point out the neon reflections
stippling the sidewalk.

Housman Prize 1998

SONG OF THE SENSES
Taos Pueblo New Mexico

I see a white-pine tree
  high on morning's horizon

I hear the wind
  that comes calling over the noon plain

I smell the river mist
  smoky with evening fires

I touch your love
  in the secret of the night

I taste I taste
  these remembered pleasures

NEW MEXICO SUNDOWN

Why should I think of you tonight,
Owl-brother, waking
from disturbed dreams
in the black cold of an English
December?

Why should my mind leap
a mile high to mountains
above the Rio Grande,
smell wet earth amid the resined
pines in that crazy world
where we watched green and orange
sunsets flame over the desert
yet invited snowmen
to our barbecue – gas-fired
you'll remember: 'High
on peppered steak,' as you put it,
'but low on smoke signals.'?

Wily Navajo
in checkered shirt and jeans,
only the owl pellet
with its mummified claw
of mousefoot, slung on a dry thong
round your throat, showing
you were no cowpoke,
that once you'd laid your blanket
on the ground.

Elder of your tribe,
stealing into my troubled night,
I try to dismiss you in favour

of much-needed sleep, try
to suppress the restless thought
coming back from a nine-years-old
conversation under the first hot stars
of a desert evening: 'You will know
before daybreak,' you told me,
'the day that I am dead.'

I await, wakeful, the dawn.

Richard Burton Award 1992

CLUTCHING . . .

. . . amber
traced at sunrise
inner cloud lining
diffused from east
windsurfing

rocks slicked
by roadside along
Grand Canyon trail
stopping for photographs

Rolling Rock lukewarm
in noonday heat
raised to our lips
wishing for cooler

sundown over North Rim
those tinted pictures
we didn't believe
printed in evidence

moon rising
larger than Mojave
images of forever
blowing our minds

MEXICAN HAT ROCK
For Dominic

Rising at 4 am. allows
an hour's climb before
the desert switches
a stoplight on our crazed
   activity.

Already sands run
menstrual red in sunrise
and chill lick of
nightbreeze turns to a mere
   tepidity.

Hunched in his stone shawl,
sombrero hooding day's advance,
back to the sun, Ol' Mex
deliberately postures reluctance
   to arise.

Our Dodge parked in shade
of outcrop, six-pack
parked in shade of Dodge –
we know a dodge or two we
   ol' timers –

we commence our climb.
My son, on athlete's limbs,
tickles rib and shoulder
as he spiders to sit astride
   Ol' Mex's ear,

deaf ol' man who hears
scarce anything, sees
even less till sleep-swaddled
eyes clear suddenly on shapes
   new-grown

overnight, greenbirth bursting
everywhere, an agency of green
on red and we the probes who cease
our climb to spacewalk in this new
   dimension.

Navajo valley cocks crow
reminding of dayblaze fast
approaching and we still pottering
in a firmament of rare
   vivacity.

Our tyremarks trail toward
the highway, rearview mirror glimpse
of Ol' Mex, brim tilted further,
gardener gazing with impassive pride
   upon his garden.

BINOCULARS

Birdwatchers use them
to tell linnet from twite

Race-goers urge their losing bets
in close-up agony

Neighbours ogle
frolicsome bedrooms.

Binoculars have their uses
magnifying

the dullness of lives
viewed through lenses

but not for my kids.
I remember their horrific glee

plunging down ice roads
out of Yellowstone

eyes focused on corners
dropping sheer into deep pine

flying fearsomeness
before we hit the bend

screaming play-terror
as our future accidents

drew near before their time
which of course they never did.

As the Sleeping Giant stirred
and blinked in their prisms

on the road to Cody
where the snows finally melted

they put the binoculars away
since it's so much safer

to meet bull elk more or less
their normal size

while we sought the sanctuary
of an edge-of-town motel.

But it sure as hell
                      was dull.

SAN FRANCISCO SOIRÉE

Nico the dysfunctional mouse
comes to dinner

On the whole
he prefers Mexican food

He arrives still wearing
his mouse costume

Which I find disconcerting
in my house

OK for McLaren Park
or even his own apartment

But not in my house
though I do see

That inviting also
Zarto the white rabbit

Sets a kind of precedent
and my friend Olissa

The marmoset has become
one of the family so to speak

I give them nachos
and Ocean Steam beer

And open a bottle
of port brought from England

We toast Sir Francis Drake
and later I read them my poems

You try reading yours sometime
to a permanently bewildered mouse

A rabbit with a crack habit
and a marmoset on the game

See if you feel you have achieved
literary fulfilment

MY LIFE IN THE MOVIES

The bronze-blond boy in the parking lot
puts down the oscar he's polishing
takes my car keys

Sun or shade backing up
Shade I say
That's ten dollars extra

The bronze-blond boy waiter
at the coffee shop
hands me a latte
Not there as I move
to a table on the patio
*can't you see
it's reserved for the Fondas*

Tourists tramp past Graumann's
get themselves photographed
placing their hands
in Marilyn's palm
or stepping on Astaire's toes

I walk down Sunset
turn off the boulevard
into sun-trap side streets
where old ladies emerge
fragile as manicures
from art deco bungalows
parading their pink-dyed poodles
*Don' cha know young man
I was once a star*

Moonrise over Malibu
living the movie life
rolling my Dodge
with its bent fender
to the ocean's edge

Stopped on the parkway
I choose a beachbar
where the young bronze-blond bartender
beams a smile bright
as a piña colada

Get outa here dumbo
can't you see
we're shooting
this ain't a bar
you're on our f**king set

MALIBU BLUES

Maybe I'll come home now
Maybe I'll stop by
Maybe sun'll rise tomorrow
Maybe a blue sky

Sad refrain from a beachbar
jukebox long ago
only half-remembered
in the twilight afterglow

Come down to the harbour
where the tides unwind
find flotsam and find jetsam
of a human kind

Between the gold of waking
and the dull pearl of sleep
the rain keeps on falling
and the seabirds weep

Time spent in the bar-room
waiting for your call
doesn't seem to signify
how the dice will fall

Come hope and high water
the white sail and the black
it hits my mind like seaspray
you're never coming back

LAST TREE TO PARIS

*A journey of a thousand miles
begins with a single step*
        Lao Tzu

At 4 am. lamplight slanted
in bars through oak branches,

fireflies of drizzle flitted
between light and shade.

Perhaps the driver had forgotten
and I'd have to walk to Paris.

I tested the weight of my suitcase
the waterproofing of my coat,

stood further under the tree
leaning against the trunk.

The cab arrived of course
the train, the boat and Paris.

That was over thirty years ago
and since then so many thousand miles,

but always somewhere on each journey
an oak tree to offer comfort.

SVENDBORG REMEMBERED
For Else & Lars

That evening you told me
of the day the black barn
burned in the empty field
and the villages had
no music in them
though the earth was warm
and the dew span in rivers,
pouring down to the silent
uncomplaining *Baelt*.

Your umber house
lay low beside the road
and the lights were out,
the strong grass spiking easily
through the turf thatch,
purple and powerless,
the crooked frame rotting,
blotched with the rust
of the vanished nail.

Now hope like a dancer
has brought you an infant
to skip in unmeasured time
beyond this century
of wars and occupations

and I drive away across
your pine-planked bridge,
waving farewell amid chestnuts
burning their new-lit candles.

Baelt: a sea strait

SOMME

I think of these things
oh I think of these many things
gliding at our regulation
100 kilometres per hour
across the valley of the Somme
this Friday afternoon.

Here where the A1
crosses the valley at Feuillères
there are leavings indeed
first leavings of spring
and another leaving
of a different kind,

a budding of mottled bones
beneath isolated crosses in fields
of trench-by-trench headstones
drilled to readiness for inspection
in the country churchyards
of Frise Clery and Hem-Monacu.

And I give a kind of thanks
for my own existence made possible
by the fact my father does not lie here
as he might so easily have done
under the heavy loam now springing
its new season's wheat

because a German stretcher party,
captives now forced to serve their foe,
chose to treat him like a brother
picking his shattered limbs
from the rubble of battle

to deliver him from evil,

pressing into his unconscious hand
the matchbox I still have
that he would know upon waking
the Bosch gave him the light
for his first cigarette of survival
and a family as yet unborn,

wishing him brotherhood
from one who had to be an enemy,
that match ignited by the trigger
of war ordained by unnamed politicians
safe in the plush of their hotels
rolling their nightly dice.

Today the Somme is good for fishing
according to the road sign
and sure enough there rides
a blunt-nosed punt in which,
with unlit Gauloise and a carbon rod,
reclines a fisherman.

BUYING CHOCOLATE

We are the border patrol
tourists stopping
to buy chocolates
somewhere in no man's land
on a vague Euro-frontier
marked only by redundant
customs posts

To one side a Belgian canal
regulates there shall be
no turning that way
as sentinel herons fish
still as tombstones
now that no smugglers
come by

To the other a settlement
of newly-varnished sheds
adorns allotments
on a French township boundary
each tended plot
pushing up its green bush
of young spring crops

Unobtrusive
in the last field of Flanders
lies one small rectangle
where stone crosses mark
those who tramped and bled
into this ever-fallow earth
seeds of an everlasting harvest

ANAMNESIS

Poppies on a hot summer night
and a distant radio

You have seen and heard
you have seen and heard these too

A menu written in Greek
English and French

You have read this
and a waiter has taken your order

Has bowed over a circular table
and scribbled on a pale green pad

The first long glance of the wine
is surely the best

The iron bite of the wine on the tongue
is unforgettable

We flick through the pages
of magazines

With fingers that already feel the curl
of the rheumatic worm

We give it momentary recognition
you and I

Before we banish it totally
or at least for tonight

Tune to other pulses of reassurance
between the two of us

Poppies on a hot summer night
and a distant radio

AFTER PIRAEUS
For E.H.

We left when Uncle Leonidas said
there were only olives, no more meat
and the last headless chicken
stopped quaking.

Mama is tired, Mama coughs up dust,
the fishermen who step over us
have fish scales
stuck to the soles of their feet.

In Kalabaka seagulls dive
in the hour before dark
squabbling over squid,
their wings burnt by the setting sun.

Mama holds out her hand
for *lepta,*
the dogs come and grin at us
and the men give her red wine.

I do not know about death
or why I did not weep when they told me,
I only remember a finger pointing
and hands lifting me up.

On the aeroplane
I sleep most of the journey
and only feel like crying
when someone asks me
if I have been dreaming.

Short-listed for the Frogmore Prize 1996

MEMORIAL DAY

The village square baked to white dust
beetles scurrying to protect
the cochineal cases of their wings

The sun beats on the fountain
dribbling its tepid wine into the silence
into the stillness

The old man sits beneath the fountain
his jacket folded beside him his hat removed
his waistcoat unbuttoned

He is waiting for the cornets and the sousaphone
the rap of polished boots the kicked up dust
the rat-a-tat and clash of the cymbals

He stands to caress the creases from his shirt
tries to remember the time they came
for his father maybe his son

and shakes his fist

The musicians halt and lower their instruments
the captain waits
his hand on the hilt of his sword

Wearily as if another year
has passed much too quickly
the old man slowly salutes

HOMAGE TO EDWARD HOPPER
1882-1967

They stand
at open windows
or sit
on brownstone stoops
gather late
in all night bars
or simply watch
the sun rise
over empty streets

Often in twos
threes or fours
always alone
gazing beyond
their here and now
seeking escape
from the hurt of being
forever bound
by the picture's frame

STANDING BACK
Photograph: LS Lowry at Salford College of Art 1927

Pencil and brush articulate
the thought co-ordinating
hand and eye. Eager students
hunch over board and easel,
peer at the model, her disdainful
gaze half-turned from them,
boredom transcribing her form,
tight in white gaiters
and military tunic, relief
and a Sobranie cigarette
still half an hour away.

Lowry stands back:
in a corner of the room,
his angle easily the worst,
hand on hip he does not paint
but gazes at her
with reflective purpose
feeling no urge to paint;
storing instinctively
all the painting yet to come
in the long years
of the rest of his life.

AT THE BATHING HOUSE
Kitagawa Utamaro: *The Handtowel* 1802/04

Walk with me
along the path to the bathing house
the air is fragrant
with pear blossom

And yet you hesitate
the admonitions of the poet
worry you
his praise of places
anywhere far from here

What cheek
he even likens me
to the mortuary of Tokugawa
which is why I turn my shoulder
putting his words behind me
invisible as night snow
falling on distant mountains

Come closer
regard the silk of my bathrobe
how its folds will caress me
as it slips from my body
feel the soft flax
of my handtowel
pampered with rose oil
how it will comfort your wet skin

Remember the poet says
I am cute as a charnel temple
for nothing
is more honourable
than to pay homage
to one's ancestors

SUCH AN UGLY SUBJECT
Ford Madox Ford: *An English Autumn Afternoon* 1852/54

We come here Wednesdays about 3
   my half day
When she has a couple of hours
   between lunch and tea
To look at the view and chat
   no more than that

Trees just starting to turn
   burnished in October light
Hampstead spread out before us
   the world at our feet
Highgate a distant spire
   smoke from a garden fire

Down there late apple-pickers
   play throw and catch
With the last russet fruit of the year
   voices carried on Autumn air
If only I could paint all this
   preserve our few moments of bliss

'Such an ugly subject'
   that fellow Ruskin says
'No interest no romance
   not worth painting at all
too suburban too bleak'
   but he doesn't have to meet just once a week

THE CRITICS
Harold Harvey: *The Critics* 1922

Glass of crême de menthe
untouched on the table
she glances nervously
fingertips tapping cheek
awaiting their verdict

Notes Ella's hands
on Gertrude's shoulders
knows she has already
made up her mind
has seen it all before

Watches Gertrude hesitate
disdain on her lips
becoming a hint of a smile
searching for words
to soften the blow

Fledgling artist trapped
Ella ready to be resolute
Gertrude longing
to knock back
the rest of her kirsch

If only someone
would descend the stairs
seen through the open door
the painter himself perhaps
who with a stroke
could release them all

SOUTHWOLD 1937
Stanley Spencer

Bathing suits
flap flip
on a makeshift
drying line
above deckchairs
lounging empty mostly
black and
orange stripes
facing the crumbling
waves

That year
I am born
my mother
tending me
all through
the summer's heat
pushing me daily
on our nursery
excursions
to the beach

Spencer knowing
none of this
searches for precise umbers
among pebbles
though the black
veneer of my pram
attracts him
and he must care
somewhat for
mother's orange hat

GREEN CHILDREN (2)
The *Green Child* paintings of
Conroy Maddox 1939 and Oscar Mellor 1950

They are everywhere
the green children
they laugh at us
from the tops of trees
(we always forget to look up
or we'd see them laughing at us)

We who were once green children
only sometimes remember
we once had a green child for a friend
one who never came back
whom we yearn to meet more
and more in the remaining hours
of our dwindling lives

Remember the one
you said goodbye to
by an open window
your eye caught by the curtain
shifting in the breeze
at the moment of leaving
so that when you looked again
they were gone
and gone forever

The boy with the violin
you waved away
from the station platform
watching the train thin its way
round the curve of the track

The girl whose hand you held
for so long at the airport
who was gone in the wink of an eye
till the airplane banked into cloud
and there was no eye to wink back

Green children
loves that cannot age
who laugh at us
and grow moths' wings
to fly by moonlight
wavering through time
back to the empty lighthouse
called memory

We who think we are
the sum of our observable parts
yet who are no more
than molecules of a greater mass
which floats its fragments
through the interstices of space
catching the timbre of the spheres

till the moth wings converge
on a chosen trajectory we cannot calibrate
spiralling in a time we cannot predict
to fuse and forge a new green child

CHERRY BEND CREEK
Bridget Riley: *Cherry Autumn* 1983

Leelanau was always Cherry County
in upstate Michigan
Traverse City hosting
the National Cherry Festival
summer stock opening the season
in Cherry County Playhouse

That autumn we drove to Leland
(still 'autumn' not 'fall' in Cherry County)
after the festival was over
stopped to picnic under sun sliding
in bars through maples
bordering Cherry Bend Creek
water running streaked with pinks
and ambers of fallen leaves

At Leland Quay sail boats
slapped against posts
tied along the board walk
dried-out planking
drumming with footfall
as children screamed their
don't-step-in-the-crack laughter
peering through splintered gaps
at waves swimming side-stroke
around the anchoring stays

Over on Sleeping Bear Dune
domes and pockets of sand
hove ursine flanks
wind off the lake scuffing skin-dry
grass and grain on the snuffling shore

Vapour trails chalked blueboard of sky
as jets burned down to Chicago
over Lake Michigan
and we bought the last of the cherry pulp
oozing juice between teeth
to dribble down stained chins
parallel trickles of fun

After sundown
ripening wind stirred memories
blew more grit onto beach fires
charcoaling steaks
moon rising over lake
singing ballads in owl language
requiem for the Edward Fitzgerald
largest lake carrier ever
sunk under the turbulence
of a land-locked ocean storm
sailors' skulls still keening
somewhere beneath us
under star-spinning waters
as our guitars played on

Later while some tucked fatigue
into sleeping bags
on Sleeping Bear
we put out in silent canoes
to paddle the night along Cherry Bend
our torches catching eyes
peering from banded darkness
along river banks striped like awnings
mauve and ochre bars intervalled
with white moon-ribbons of memory
spaces through which the mind
taking off on its own private journeys
was able to slip at will

LIKE AN OPEN BOOK
Howard Hodgkin: *Like an Open Book* 1990

Like an open book
I am here to be read
pages giving expression
to thoughts described
by the brush not the pen

Like an open book
you must read me singly
I cannot speak
to more than one of you
at any given time

Like an open book
I am open to misunderstanding
or perhaps being understood
too well for which
I am apt to be burnt

Like an open book
I am written and rewritten
painted and repainted
read and re-read
my message volatile

Like an open book
you see me now
pages riffled by the wind
sunlight blazing as much
from within as without

Hodgkin writes: 'I believe that, as an artist, I can only speak to one person at a time.'

TROUBLE AT A TAVERN
After Dafydd ap Gwilym fl. 1340-70

I came to a fair city,
My trusty squire behind me,
Sought out a worthy hostel
And, with no thought of cost
(I was ever rash with money),
Lashed out on food and drink.

I spied a slim, fair virgin
(Oh, what rapture) sitting alone
and, falling at once in love,
Invited her to my table.
How coy she was, how reluctant,
Yet, once her fears were overcome,
How she quaffed the costly wines,
How tucked into the great roast.

And thus I dared whisper
Words of quiet enticement,
Made tryst to come to her chamber
While all the company slept;
Ah, those black brows I longed to kiss.

When at last all were abed
I, on tiptoe, did commence
My silent journey to her side
But, on a sudden, tripped –
How easy to be clumsy –
And, stumbling forward, lurched
Into a loud and stupid stool,
Left by the careless ostler,
Upon which I barked my shin.

Which would not have been so bad
Had I not, in trying to balance,
Put out my hand to grasp
the table edge which tilted,
Sending metal platters
and iron pots a-clattering
And, being on trestles resting,
Did cause the legs to fall,
So that all the boards in turn
Around the room came crashing.

Which would not have been so bad
Had not I in alarm recoiled
Backwards into the dresser
Which, standing upon an uneven flag,
Tilted forward showering me
With tankards and pans
And all manner of pewter,
Which made great din upon the stone.

Which would not have been so bad
Had not this set the dogs to barking,
Waking those three English scum,
Hickin and Jenkin and Jack,
Who cursed aloud and roared:
'Beware that accursed Welshman
Is on the prowl to rob us.'
Whereon the ostler, leaping up,
Aroused all the other guests
Who set to with hue and cry.

Which would not have been so bad
Had not the racket frightened
The horses in their stable
Who whinnied and kicked their stalls,
Alarming the oxen bedded nearby
Which bellowed mightily, setting
The sheep in the fold to bleating
And the scurvy geese to honking,
Bringing all abed in the street
To their windows and doors,
Who halloo'd their neighbours
In mutual hullabaloo.

Which would not have been so bad
Had not the very elements
Seemingly been disturbed
And a great wind rising
Smacked and clattered
The shutters and casements
And thunder, raging
Through the heavens, seemed
To rent the very earth in twain.

Which would not have been so bad
Had not my dearest darling
Come next morning to breakfast,
Seeming to see me not, yet contriving
To crush her heel into my toe
Upon passing my chair,
The meanwhile favouring
Our greasy, loathsome landlord
With simpering nods and smiles,
Saying how refreshed was she,

How deeply she had slumbered,
As should become a virgin
Sleeping at night alone
In such a peaceful inn.

POSTSCRIPT
TAKE-DOWN

I am the clown
I am last night's show
but you will not know that

I have wiped
the painted stars
from my eyes

Perhaps I am the pony
you rode to the show
only no one knows

The poodle parading
on hind legs only
old habits die hard

I live above your head
beneath your feet
a knot in the lace

of your shoe
if you care
to untie me

I look for you looking
through the circle
of your garden window

I climb the stair
to pull back the ratchets
to unlock the shutters

I ramble the 5 acre meadow
at sunrise my footprints
dappled with dew

I trace a path
that becomes a story
a fable of distances

a trail beside the river
we might have taken
once in the very long

With thanks to Jo Shapcott: Ledbury Festival 1998